Original title:
Bananas in Bloom

Copyright © 2025 Creative Arts Management OÜ
All rights reserved.

Author: Simon Fairchild
ISBN HARDBACK: 978-1-80586-302-1
ISBN PAPERBACK: 978-1-80586-774-6

Whispers of Ripeness

In the garden, green and bright,
A fruit that laughs in morning light.
With spots of yellow, such a show,
They giggle softly as they grow.

Peeling layers, what a tease!
Birds around it sing with ease.
In a fruit bowl, snug and round,
They launch their jokes without a sound.

Audacious Curves

Curvy shapes that twist and bend,
In the sun, they like to send.
With a wink, they take their stand,
A fruity joke, oh isn't it grand?

Bumping noses in the breeze,
They swing and twirl with such great ease.
All the critters pause to stare,
At the fruit so bold; they dare!

Oasis of Flavor

In a world of gray and gloom,
A yellow smile begins to bloom.
With laughter echoing in the air,
They bring delight with fruity flair.

Sipping nectar with a friend,
Jokes and laughter never end.
In the shade, they throw a dance,
Rolling giggles; what a chance!

Tidal Waves of Sweetness

Swirling twists upon the tide,
In every crevice, joy will hide.
With each nibble, giggles start,
A chuckle from the juicy heart.

Splashing flavors everywhere,
Tickling taste buds, do beware!
A fruity wave that jolts the day,
In silly fun, they love to play.

Echoes of Sweetness

In a land where fruits can dance,
Laughing leaves in sun's bright glance.
Joyful peels start to play along,
Swinging softly like a song.

Mister Monkey swings with glee,
A fruit feast as wild as can be.
He tiptoes on a leafy stage,
Shouting loud, 'Let's cause some rage!'

Beneath the Sun's Gaze

Golden orbs in rowdy cheer,
Sunlight dances, make way, clear!
With every twist, a giggle grows,
Tickling tops like funny shows.

Silly snails in shades of green,
Trying out a fruit routine.
Who knew green could be such fun?
When we laugh, we all have won!

Garden of Endless Possibilities

In a jungle bursting bright,
Puns are ripe, it feels just right.
Each vine is tangled, full of glee,
Whispers of what could be free.

Chatter of the playful bugs,
Swapping tales with silly shrugs.
In this patch, life's a delight,
Giggle through the day and night.

Fertile Earth Awakened

Wake up soil with laughter's might,
Sprouting jokes from left to right.
Roots are tickled, worms do a twist,
Join the fun, you can't resist!

In this patch of cheeky fun,
Everyone's under the sun.
Grow a smile, share a chuckle,
Nature's laughter is quite a huddle.

Brightness Entwined

In green hats, they strut with flair,
A cheerful bunch beyond compare.
Swinging low with silly grins,
Time for fruit, let the fun begin!

They giggle in the sunlit grove,
A dance of joy, oh how they move!
With laughter tangled in the breeze,
Happiness sways among the leaves.

Nature's Gestation

Beneath the sun, a journey starts,
With leafy wigs and yellow hearts.
They wiggle and they sway with glee,
What charming sights for all to see!

Funky forms with shapes so grand,
A sight that tickles where we stand.
In playful clusters, packed so tight,
Nature's jokes bring pure delight.

Unfolding Ecstasy

A peep show from the leafy beds,
What fruit pranks dance inside their heads?
In playful whispers, they confess,
A fruity circus, nothing less!

The punchlines drop like autumn leaves,
Each ripe surprise, oh how it cleaves!
In giggles sweet, they claim their space,
With happy faces—such a chase!

Tropical Glee

In tropic sun, the merry crew,
With smiles bright and colors true.
They bounce around in merry haste,
A fruity feast with no time to waste!

Like little suns, they shine so bright,
Their playful charm is pure delight.
In every corner, joy erupts,
As nature's fruit hilariously jumps!

Sweet Potential Unfurled

In a pantry bright, yellow and bold,
Swaying gently, their stories unfold,
Each peel a promise, a giggle, a grin,
Who knew such laughter could grow from within?

Bunches of joy hang high in the breeze,
Enticing a taste, with such simple ease,
A slip of a peel, oh what a delight,
Comedic spills bring laughter at night.

Nature's Kaleidoscope

In gardens aglow with colors galore,
Funny shapes dance, oh what's in store?
Curves and contours, a fruity parade,
Nature's own jesters, unafraid.

Under sun's wink, they curve with a cheer,
Each twist a chuckle, drawing us near,
Green to the gold, a vibrant display,
A fruity fiesta in full-blown array.

The Art of Ripening

With each passing day, they take on the glow,
From emerald dreams to a mellow yellow,
Jokes in their sweetness, ripe for a bite,
A play on our senses, oh what a sight!

Hanging out in bunches, they gibe and tease,
Softening secrets carried by the breeze,
A mash of good humor, on fruit stands they sit,
Ready to chuckle, with every sweet bit.

Verdant Dreams Unraveled

In the jungle's heart, they dangle and sway,
Whispers of laughter, brightening the day,
Chasing the sun, they wiggle with glee,
A whimsical charm from the tall, leafy tree.

With every twist, a quirky surprise,
Yellow delights that bring chuckles and sighs,
Dancing in sunlight, a comical scene,
Fruity mischief where joy reigns supreme.

Golden Curves and Leafy Whispers

In the garden, they wiggle with glee,
Golden curves hanging from every tree.
Leaves sway gently, a playful cheer,
Mischief lurking, one tickle, they leer.

Sunshine laughs, casting shadows below,
Whispers of sweetness, a secret show.
Chasing each other on a breeze's tune,
Gladly they bounce, like a jolly cartoon.

Tropical Sunlight on Rippling Green

Sunlight dances on emerald leaves,
Tickling the fruit that the warm air weaves.
Giggles escape with each playful sway,
Nature's jesters, brightening the day.

With a wink, they blush in the heat,
Jokingly hiding, oh what a feat!
Under the warmth, the laughter erupts,
A tropical scene where joy never interrupts.

The Dance of Yellow Petals

Yellow petals are little jesters at play,
Spinning and twirling, they brighten the day.
Cackling softly, they float on the breeze,
A comic parade through the warm summer leaves.

Each twirl brings laughter, a whimsical sight,
They tease the sun with their vibrant delight.
In a garland of joy, they celebrate true,
Nature's own punsters, a colorful crew.

Under the Canopy of Sweetness

Under the canopy, sweet secrets bloom,
Laughter and jests fill the delightful room.
Playful whispers dance in the air,
A symphony of joy, none can compare.

Leaves rustle softly, with chuckles and cheer,
Chasing away every shadow of fear.
In this tropical land where fun comes alive,
Each twist and turn makes the heart truly thrive.

Sunlit Cascades

In the garden, giggles rise,
With yellow hats 'neath sunny skies.
A slip, a trip, oh what a sight,
As fruit takes flight in pure delight.

Monkeys swing with cheeky cheer,
Chasing shadows, drawing near.
The laughter dances through the air,
While sunshine plays without a care.

Golden Curves of Joy

Wobbling fruits in bright parade,
Jellybeans with sunshine made.
Round and plump, they roll so free,
Creating chaos, oh, my glee!

A peal of laughter, slippery ends,
As fruity folly never bends.
With giggles blooming all around,
Joyful antics know no bounds.

Orchard's Lush Embrace

Amidst the leaves, a silly hub,
As frolicsome friends share their grub.
With every munch, a laugh erupts,
In fruity games, all joy corrupts.

Sunbeams flicker, shadows play,
Chasing critters on their way.
Each sunny chuckle spins and twirls,
In this patch, where joy unfurls.

Harvesting Sunshine

Up in the trees, the jokes collide,
With zany tales that twist and glide.
As punchlines drop like ripened fruit,
The orchard fills with laughter's loot.

Gathering smiles, we skip and hop,
   No one's worried if we flop.
In this fair ground of breezy cheer,
We feast on giggles, loud and clear.

Mellow Harmony

In a garden where laughter grows,
Round fruits wear smiles, trying to pose.
Swaying gently in the sun's bright sheen,
Nature's jesters dressed in vivid green.

The squirrels chuckle, swinging so high,
While crickets play tunes, oh me, oh my!
With every giggle, plants start to sway,
In this merry dance, life finds its way.

Whirling in Abundance

A jolly bunch spins round and round,
With a zany dance beneath the ground.
Their laughter bubbles up to the trees,
Swirling joy on a soft, warm breeze.

They wear polka dots in the golden sun,
Each one a character, each one some fun.
Tickled leaves rustle, giving a cheer,
As roots wiggle wildly, bringing good cheer.

Melody of Green

In a leafy realm where giggles bloom,
Fruits hum sweet songs as they find their room.
A tangle of vines with playful intent,
Whispering secrets of joy that they scent.

The shadows dance like a silly parade,
With figures of laughter, none are afraid.
In this vibrant world, silly and bright,
Good humor and nature share pure delight.

Nature's Sweet Embrace

Bouncing brightly in the garden's heart,
Chasing sunlight, each day a new start.
Watch them wiggle, twist, and cheer,
Fruity charm, bringing us near.

With giggles and wiggles, they strike a pose,
Nature's merry jesters, everyone knows.
The earth shakes with laughter, pure and divine,
In this fruitful circle, all life intertwines.

The Aroma of Growth

In the jungle, a scent so sweet,
A treat that's hard to beat.
Green giants wave in the breeze,
Tickling noses with such ease.

Leaves rustle with a playful sigh,
As curious critters scamper by.
Nature's laughter, pure delight,
Dancing shadows in the light.

Fruitful dreams, a sunny tale,
Underneath the leafy veil.
Bunches eager to break free,
Oh, what joy they bring to me!

In the heart of sunny glades,
Miracles dressed in leafy shades.
Let's feast on this wild show,
With every breeze, our spirits grow.

Embrace of the Tropics

In a land where sunshine plays,
Surprises sprout on golden days.
Round and ripe, they swing and sway,
Nature's jesters in the fray.

With laughter lines on every peel,
They charm us with their fruity zeal.
A comedy on branches spun,
In the spotlight, they have fun!

Characters clad in vibrant hue,
Whispering secrets old and new.
Under the sun, they mock and tease,
Swaying gently with the breeze.

Their giggles fill the air with cheer,
A carnival we hold so dear.
In every twist and every turn,
A juicy jest, our hearts will yearn.

Fragile Petals Dance

Petals flutter, soft as lace,
Nature's waltz, a gentle race.
Twirling whispers in the sky,
A floral ballet, oh so spry.

In the breeze, they dip and dive,
A fleeting chance to feel alive.
Every bob, a silly jest,
In colorful gowns, they are dressed.

Swaying low on slender stems,
Playing hide and seek with hems.
Giggling, gossiping, in delight,
With each new dawn, a fresh invite.

And when the evening paints the sky,
They dance until the stars are nigh.
A party in the dusky room,
Laughter echoing through the gloom.

Cloak of Emerald

In a vast and leafy cloak,
A vibrant joke, it's no hoax.
Emerald arms stretch wide and bright,
A grand backdrop for laughter's light.

Twists and turns, a playful maze,
Where critters waddle, hop and gaze.
Hiding spots of mirth galore,
Behind each leaf, what's in store?

Funny shapes amid the green,
Unexpected sights seldom seen.
Every rustle holds a grin,
A chuckle shared on gentle skin.

The sunbeams break with silly glee,
A jester's court beneath the tree.
In this realm where laughter blooms,
We find ourselves in funny rooms.

Gold Dust Among the Leaves

In the jungle, gold treasures peek,
Yellow guards play hide and seek.
Twisting vines in a playful dance,
Funny fruits in a sunny prance.

Swinging low, they jive and sway,
Smiles erupt at their fun display.
Chasing monkeys, with cheeky glee,
Nutty giggles from each leafy tree.

Sipping nectar, sweet and bright,
Silly critters share delight.
As sunlight sprinkles, laughter grows,
Nature's joy, a vibrant shows.

Golden treasures on every branch,
Join the fun, come take a chance!
Under a sunbeam's playful beam,
Life's a wacky, fruity dream!

Fruity Fantasia in the Shade

In a leafy spot where shadows play,
Fruity friends come out to sway.
Dancing leaves in the summer breeze,
Whispering secrets with such ease.

Jolly bunches in vibrant hues,
Playing pranks, sharing news.
Tickling vines, they giggle loud,
An absurdity that makes us proud.

Napping critters in soft repose,
Dream of sweetness, how it flows.
With each burst of laughter shared,
Life's a treat, oh how we dared!

Colors splash in silly spree,
Jumping joyfully, wild and free.
In this fruity realm we play,
Giggles linger, come what may!

The Embrace of Warmth and Growth

Amidst the green, a warm embrace,
Fruits of joy put on a face.
Beneath the sun, their laughter gleams,
Chasing sunshine, like sweet dreams.

Leaves are tickled by the breeze,
Nature's laughter brings us ease.
Wobbly fruits in jolly cheer,
Nature's fun is always near.

Roots entwined in playful hug,
Amid the vines, joy gives a tug.
In the garden, a bright surprise,
Nature's whimsy, dancing skies.

Friendship blooms in vibrant zones,
Jolly sounds from leafy groans.
In this world of sunny sights,
We find laughter, soft delights!

A Canvas of Flavorful Vibrance

Under a canvas kissed by sun,
Flavorful fun has just begun.
Colors splash in gleeful arcs,
Whirlwind laughter, little sparks.

Sketches formed in yellow shades,
Silly dances, leafy parades.
Witty whispers from every tree,
Painting joy for you and me.

Ticklish fruits in a playful row,
Stealing glances, come and go.
Frolicking under skies so bright,
A banquet of giggles, pure delight!

Each tasty bite, a story spun,
With every munch, more joy begun.
In this garden of whimsy free,
Laughter's flavor, a jubilee!

Nature's Lush Celebration

In gardens where the sunbeam plays,
The fruits wear sunny, cheerful shades.
With laughter shared on breezy days,
Each twist and turn, a joy cascades.

The leaves, they dance in playful glee,
A jungle tune from bumble bees.
With fuzzy squawks from nearby trees,
Nature sings with such wild ease.

Between the blossoms, mirth does bloom,
Where critters leap and never gloom.
In nature's funny, grand costume,
We gather 'round, dispelling gloom.

A fragrant feast where smiles abound,
In lush embrace, we twirl around.
For every fruit, a laughter sound,
In harmony, our joys are found.

Yellows and Greens in Harmonious Chorus

In fields of gold, the giggles rise,
A jester's cap, the fruit disguised.
Beneath the branches, watch the skies,
With painted hues, the sun complies.

The leaves whisper secrets light and free,
As critters parade in a row we see.
Bouncing about, what could they be?
A fruity fest, a jubilee!

With every squeeze and sticky hand,
We summon joy across the land.
In nature's court, both bright and grand,
We laugh together, oh so planned!

Through yellows bold and greens so bright,
We spin and twirl from morn to night.
In the orchard's arms, what pure delight,
We gather 'round, a joyful sight.

A Tale of Sunlit Abundance

A tale unfolds in vibrant hue,
Where sunny smiles from skies so blue.
The bounty shines, a comical view,
In every round, a laughter too.

From tree to tree, the giggles flow,
As fruits parade in a brightened show.
Bouncing here and bouncing low,
The joy in sunlit streams does grow.

With golden skins that slip and slide,
A playful chase, we run and glide.
In every corner, silly and wide,
Abundance reigns, our hearts abide.

And when the dusk transforms the scene,
We dance and laugh amidst the green.
The sweet delight, so fresh, so keen,
A tale of joy, forever serene.

The Hidden Joys of Orchard Light

In shady spots where giggles bloom,
The fruits are dressed in life's costume.
With leaves that rustle to dispel gloom,
    The orchard sings, a jolly tune.

The sun peeks through in playful beams,
As laughter spills in golden streams.
The hidden joy, it softly gleams,
Within the trees, a dance of dreams.

A chorus fills the air, so sweet,
As critters hop on tiny feet.
Each fruity guest takes to the street,
In this grand jest, we all compete!

With every pluck and giggle shared,
A moment here is fully bared.
In orchard light, we've all prepared,
To laugh together, none compared.

The Language of Lushness

In the garden bright and quirky,
Fruits donned hats quite dapper,
They speak in giggles and glee,
    Wobbling like a merry caper.

Lemonade rain and coconut cream,
Where laughter sways in the breeze,
Fruits dance in a fruity dream,
    Every bite a joke that teases.

The mango wears its crown with pride,
While avocados tell a tale,
Together they form a jolly ride,
    With giggles that never pale.

In a tropical chat, no fruit unites,
Each bite's a pun, a fruity jest,
Among the leaves and vibrant sights,
    Nature plays host to its best.

Fruitful Whispers Beneath the Palms

Underneath the swaying fronds,
Fruits plot their next big prank,
With whispers soft like gentle ponds,
They gather for a fruity prank.

A pineapple in shades so bright,
Claims it's the king of the lot,
While coconuts chuckle in delight,
Saying, 'Ha! You're just a pot!'

Papayas blush with juicy glee,
Over jokes of the banana split,
While berries giggle, 'Look at we!'
One slip, and oh, what a hit!

Every fruit has a role to play,
In this comedy of sunshine,
They role-play jokes through the day,
In laughter, they intertwine.

Tropical Whispers

In the sun where the colors burst,
Fruits share jokes, a merry crew,
Bouncing high, it's a funny thirst,
Chasing laughs as the breezes blew.

The guava grinned with rosy cheeks,
While limes told tales so bright,
From silly tricks to fruity peaks,
They danced beneath the moonlight.

Citrus served as the goofy host,
With zest that's filled with silly quirks,
Each giggle rising, like a toast,
To joyful days, with playful smirks.

In a carnival of fruity cheer,
They prance and sparkle in the air,
With every mock and every sneer,
The palms stand witness to their flair.

Fruitful Reverie

In a grove where sunshine beams,
Fruits wriggle with a funny wail,
They share their dreams and silly schemes,
On adventures that never pale.

Kiwis plot in shades of green,
Maestros of joyful jests,
In their world, they reign as queen,
With laughter at fruit-related quests.

Tropical jesters, bright and bold,
In punchlines that stretch for miles,
Their humor is rich, a sight to behold,
Bringing forth the sweetest smiles.

Among the foliage and the fun,
Every fruit, a comic star,
In this reverie, they cleverly run,
With joy that travels near and far.

Harvesting Radiance

In the garden where smiles sprout,
Little hands jump with a shout,
Golden bunches sway and tease,
Underneath the sunny breeze.

Laughter dances with the sun,
Harvest time is all in fun,
Baskets filled with joy's delight,
Carefree spirits take their flight.

Fuzzy friends in yellow suits,
Swinging high with silly hoots,
Joyful feasts and silly slips,
Nature's candy, perfect nips.

With each munch, the giggles flow,
Beneath the trees, the laughter grows,
In this place of vibrant glee,
We peel our worries, wild and free.

The Secret Life of Leaves

Whispers rustle in the green,
Tales of mischief, yet unseen,
Leaves that shimmy, sway, and bend,
Plotting pranks, they twist and send.

Hidden games beneath the sun,
Nature's comedy has begun,
With a wink, they catch the light,
In this theater, pure delight.

Dancing shadows play around,
As the gentle breeze is found,
A leaf that tickles, what a sight,
Inviting giggles, pure and bright.

Green conspirators in full bloom,
Crafting laughter in the room,
Nature chuckles, hearts will soar,
Unlocking joy forevermore.

Verdant Emotions

In the orchard, colors blend,
Where nature's laughter has no end,
Joyful greens against the blue,
Whispers tell of fun anew.

Jubilant jests in every shade,
Leaves are laughing, none afraid,
Crinkled edges bring a cheer,
As life unfolds, we draw near.

With the breeze, a ticklish tease,
Mysteries swayed among the trees,
Nature's pranks, they play their role,
Creating giggles, wise and whole.

Emotions swirl in vibrant hues,
A canvas where our glee imbues,
In this realm of vivid charm,
We take a trip, no need for alarm.

Vibrations of Flavor

In the kitchen, dreams arise,
Fruity notes will mesmerize,
With a swing, we blend and mix,
Crafting potions, silly tricks.

Laughter bubbles in the pot,
A symphony of silly thought,
Sprinkling sweetness, spice, and cheer,
Every taste will draw us near.

A slice of humor, bright and spry,
Whimsical dishes pile up high,
A feast of giggles on each plate,
Whirling flavors, oh, so great!

Chopping, stirring, all in fun,
Together as we laugh and run,
In this kitchen of delight,
We savor joy, a tasty bite.

Nectar of Life

In jungles where the monkeys swing,
Peeling joy from each bright thing,
A fruitful harvest, sweet surprise,
With laughter painted in the skies.

The chatter of the bright green leaves,
Jokes are bubble-wrapped in thieves,
From tree tops high, they play their game,
A fruit so funny, never lame.

With pops and cracks in every bite,
Nature's joke, a sheer delight,
In sun-kissed laughter, we all leap,
Fruitful folly, joys to reap.

So gather round, take hearty scoops,
In fruity dances, join the troops,
For every grin and giggle shared,
Life's sweet nectar is declared.

Unveiling Hidden Treasures

In shadows cast by twisted vines,
A treasure trove, as nature pines,
Gold and yellow, peeping through,
A wonderland, all fresh and new.

Peel back layers of the day,
What's beneath is here to play,
With puns and giggles, come unwind,
The sweetest secrets you will find.

In wrinkles, folds, and silly hues,
A burst of magic, bright and true,
Each bite unfolds a funny tale,
With soft, sweet laughter on the trail.

So grab a slice, don't be shy,
Join the feast, and let joy fly,
Unveiling humor in each glance,
As we all join this rainbow dance.

Whispers of the Dark Green

In the forest where the whispers dwell,
A riddle spun, a leafy spell,
Out from shadows, yellow peeks,
With cheeky smiles, the silence speaks.

Funny critters hiding near,
In laughter's shade, they disappear,
Lurking low with playful schemes,
Wrapped in bright and leafy dreams.

Swaying softly, the branches sway,
In giggles that won't fade away,
A fruit with charm, a prankster's flair,
Poking fun into the air.

So take a chance, let humor thrive,
In nature's joke, we come alive,
With every munch and juicy drop,
The magic lingers—never stop.

Summer's Bursting Heart

When summer hits with all its might,
The garden blooms, oh what a sight,
With golden gloves, the sun bestows,
A laugh that bursts from roots below.

In fields where sunshine tends to play,
Nature's silliness holds sway,
Each fruit a jester, full of cheer,
Drawing giggles from far and near.

With every squish and playful fling,
Summer's heart begins to sing,
A melody that brings us cheer,
As fruits of fun draw us near.

So let us dance in sunlight's gleam,
Join the fruits in silly dream,
For laughter fills the summer air,
In nature's jest, we find our share.

Radiance in the Heart of the Grove

In a jungle bright with laughter,
The fruits wear smiles, oh what a chatter!
Swinging vines and silly leaps,
Nature's secret, it never sleeps.

A monkey juggles, what a clown,
With peels that dance, he twirls around.
They slip and slide with glee and cheer,
In this silly grove, there's nothing to fear.

Leaves whisper jokes in the sunny air,
As squirrels ponder life without a care.
The sunbeams giggle, the shadows play,
In this nutty world, forever they'll stay.

Beneath the laughter, a soft breeze hums,
A chorus of joy, where the fun never numbs.
Oh to roam in this jolly place,
Where nature wears a silly face.

Joyful Murmurs in a Tropical Haven

In the green hideaway, giggles abound,
Each vibrant hue brings a merry sound.
A chattering parrot drapes in delight,
While furry friends dance under the light.

Breezes tease with a playful tickle,
As vines wiggle and dance, oh so fickle!
Bright blooms burst in a colorful cheer,
Welcoming laughter, ringing so near.

The sunbeams bounce, chasing shadows away,
While critters recite their own cabaret.
With every rustle, a jest takes flight,
In this warm haven, everything feels right.

There's magic in every twirl and flip,
Where life's a carnival, come join the trip!
In this happy space, joy's easily found,
With nature's humor spinning round and round.

Nature's Golden Melody

In the orchard where the sunflowers sway,
Nuts and fruits sing in their playful way.
A giddy breeze hums a charming tune,
As squirrels strut beneath the bright moon.

Fragrant blooms laugh in the golden ray,
Juggling nectar, a sweet cabaret.
With colors bright and stories to tell,
In this joyful realm, all's unbelievably well.

Leaves clap together, a leafy applause,
As tiny critters show off their paws.
The silly chorus of nature's choir,
Carries laughter that lifts ever higher.

Glimmers of fun in every nook,
With giggles carved in each little crook.
So join the dance, let the whimsy flow,
In the golden melody of life below.

Sunkissed Wonders Hanging Low

With sunshine bathed in cheerful sheen,
The fruits dangle like jewels, bright and keen.
Each fluttering leaf whispers a joke,
As critters gather, giggling in the cloak.

The squirrels flip and tumble with flair,
While birds chirp tales of pies in the air.
Life's a banquet, no time to grumble,
In this merry splash where laughter may tumble.

Golden globes sway in the balmy breeze,
Inviting us all to join in the tease.
A dance of delight, a fanciful sight,
Where the world is painted with pure delight.

In this sunny trove, all worries cease,
Nature's comedy, a delightful piece.
So wade in the warmth, let joy flow free,
In a landscape of laughter, all spirits agree.

Fertile Blessings Beneath the Sky

In a garden of laughter, fruits grow wide,
With peels that giggle, oh what a ride!
Sunshine tickles, a fruitful parade,
Bright yellow treasures, in joy they wade.

Mischief afoot, in the orchard's cheer,
Fruits wear a crown, oh dear, oh dear!
Swinging on branches, in breezy delight,
Silly little whispers, all day and night.

The bees join the chorus, a buzz full of glee,
Pollinating punchlines, so wild and free.
Nature's comedy show, where ripeness will bloat,
In the wacky world, the fruits just joke.

So grab a ripe one, let laughter outflow,
Savor the sweetness, let silliness grow.
Under the sun's watch, a whimsical spree,
In this fruitful abyss, join the jubilee!

Eden's Sweetest Secrets

In a garden of whimsy, secrets do bloom,
Giggling fruits spill, humor in every room.
With whispers of sweetness, they plot through the day,
Crafting new jokes, in their fruity ballet.

Unearthed from shadows, with peels that can grin,
They're playing a game, and everyone's in.
Each laughter-packed bite, a whimsical treat,
Dancing with joy, with little, squishy feet.

The colors explode, a riotous scene,
Fruits plotting mischief, oh what a routine!
A punchline on branches, ripe for the cheer,
In Eden's embrace, all laughter draws near.

The fruits hold their breath, then burst into song,
A melody quirky, oh how can it be wrong?
So savor the giggles, let sweetness uplift,
In this Eden's joy, every bite is a gift!

Leafy Hands Reaching for the Sky

Upward they stretch, with leafy delight,
Reaching for giggles, oh what a sight!
Tiny green fingers dance on the breeze,
Whispering tales to the buzzing bees.

The jests fly high, in a cloud of lush green,
Where laughter and light create quite the scene.
Underneath them, the creatures all cheer,
In a leafy tableau, where fun becomes sheer.

The sun throws its rays, tickling leaves bright,
Nature's own stand-up, a whimsical sight.
As shadows play tricks on the soft, fertile ground,
The hilarity blooms, where silliness is found.

So let's sway together, in nature's good graces,
Join leafy performers, in joyous embraces.
In this verdant haven, reach for the sky,
With every laugh shared, let your spirits fly!

The Promise of Vibrant Youth

In a world full of giggles, fresh and alive,
Youthful delight makes our spirits thrive.
Chasing the daylight, with mirth's fragrant trail,
Playful and silly, on a jovial sail.

Their zest for adventure, fruitfully bold,
Stories of laughter, forever retold.
With each leap and bound, joy dances along,
In the promise of youth, where laughter is strong.

The colors are vivid, where dreams take a flight,
Silly escapades twinkle, so cheerful and bright.
Let's borrow their joy, their whimsical views,
In the chorus of youth, we'll always renew.

The fountain of laughter, an unending spree,
Life's vibrant canvas, so wild and free.
Celebrate the moments, let all troubles cease,
In the promise of youth, find your sweet peace!

Curved Elegance

In the orchard, yellow and bright,
They wave and dance, a silly sight.
Curved and twisted, they sway with glee,
Who knew fruits could be so carefree?

With hats atop, they strut around,
A festive flair, they wear the crown.
Giggling leaves and playful stems,
A botanical scene that never condemns.

Sunshine tickles, and shadows prance,
Nature's whimsy leads the dance.
From tree to tree, they make their way,
With laughter woven into the day.

So here's to the laughter that grows so high,
In a world where silliness is nigh.
With curved elegance, they surprise,
Nature's jesters under sunny skies.

Paradise Found

In a land of green, where dreams come true,
Fruit hats are donned, a vibrant hue.
Swinging in breezes, they flap and cheer,
Welcome to paradise, never fear!

Round and jolly in their big parade,
Slipping on peels, they've got it made.
With smiles so bright, they shine with glee,
Who would have thought they'd act so free?

Among the laughter, a soft refrain,
Here comes the sunshine, here comes the rain.
A contest of giggles, joys untold,
In paradise found, stories unfold.

So grab your hat, and join the fun,
Bright yellow prizes in the sun.
A fruity escapade without a care,
In this charming land, giggles fill the air.

Vibrant Tendrils

In tangled vines, a comedy grows,
With vibrant tendrils, how the laughter flows.
Each twist a chuckle, each turn a grin,
Fruits in a tangle, let the fun begin!

Up to the sky, they reach with flair,
Wobbling gently, a fruity affair.
Swaying and dancing, can you believe?
Nature's own jesters, take off your leave!

With every pluck, a joke in the air,
They giggle and wiggle without a care.
In the midst of green, their antics thrive,
Where the silly vibes truly come alive.

So swing around, don't be reserved,
In vibrant tendrils, joy is preserved.
Let laughter ripple, let spirits soar,
In this playful garden, let's explore!

A Chorus of Growth

In a sunny grove where laughter sings,
A chorus of fruits on playful swings.
Growing together in a silly show,
Each one a star with a radiant glow.

With tiny hats and big, bright grins,
They harmonize as the day begins.
Branches sway to the rhythm of cheer,
In this fruity opera, all gather near.

Twisting and twirling, oh what a spree,
Count the giggles, one, two, three!
Roots entangled, while leaves sway high,
A whimsical tune beneath the sky.

So clap your hands, the fun won't cease,
Join in the chorus, feel the peace.
In their joyful dance, let's take a ride,
With laughter and love, let's grow side by side.

Sweet Seasons

In a garden that giggles and sways,
Green giants dance in the sun's warm rays.
They wear hats made of socks, quite neat,
All the critters join in for a treat.

With vibrant smiles and peels so bright,
They play hide and seek into the night.
Chasing each other, a slip and a slide,
In this merry chaos, no need to hide!

A smoothie parade with a twist of cheer,
Everyone's invited, come close, don't fear!
And as laughter echoes, they twirl around,
In this fruity fiesta, joy knows no bound.

So grab your friends, come out and play,
The sweetness of life is just a peel away!
In the garden of giggles where fun's the theme,
Life's a ripe wonder — or is it a dream?

Enchanted Rippling

A splash of yellow hides in the vine,
Whispers of sweetness, oh how divine!
They twinkle like stars under the sky,
With a wiggle and dance, oh my, oh my!

They trade silly jokes with the bumblebee,
"Why did you buzz? To make honey glee!"
Each chuckle and chortle bounces around,
As the fruit fills the air with joy all around.

The squirrels hold hands, joining the show,
While dancing fruit winks a cheeky hello.
They roll in the grass, all giddy with zest,
In this playful place, we are truly blessed!

So grab a sombrero, let's all take a spin,
Join the parade where the fun's just begin!
Under the canopy of laughter and cheer,
Life's a wild party when friends gather near!

Green Gold

In a world where everything's fresh and bright,
Green gold emerges, a pure delight.
With their quirky shapes and happy faces,
They launch into the air, taking wild chases.

They race the breeze in a merry old game,
Each one more silly, they're never the same.
The sun's golden giggle makes ripples of fun,
As everyone joins in, oh what a run!

Their laughter's contagious, the earth spins with glee,
As they share cheerful tales beneath the tree.
A party of fruit, laughter fills the air,
In this green haven, joy is everywhere!

So come for a while and sway in the sun,
Join hands with the jollies; let's all be young!
For life's a sweet journey, no reason to frown,
In this quirky little orchard, we wear our crown!

Whirling Pools of Light

In the glimmering glow, they spin and twirl,
Bright whirls of joy in a lush, green swirl.
With laughter that dances on tipsy toes,
These cheeky delights put on vibrant shows!

They leap through the air with a bounce and a flip,
Tickling the breeze on a delightful trip.
Chasing the clouds with a giggle and grin,
Creating a ruckus, let the fun begin!

Each day they play in the golden sun,
With winks and with wiggles, oh, what fun!
The gleeful whispers echo far and wide,
In this merry land, come try the ride!

A celebration each day, let's join the cheer,
These silly sweet fruits bring everyone near.
So hop to the rhythm, let laughter ignite,
In the whirling pools of joy and light!

The Secret Life of a Fruiting Tree

In the orchard, whispers thrive,
Where the jolly fruit takes a dive.
Coconuts giggle, and apples jest,
While the citrus fruits dance, feeling blessed.

Underneath the sun's bright gaze,
The tree throws a party, it's quite the craze.
With every sway, it shakes like a clown,
Lending the breeze a whimsical gown.

Pineapples wear their crowns with pride,
Making bananas laugh as they glide.
Lemons toss confetti, oh what a sight,
As pears do the tango under moonlight.

But watch out for the rambunctious leaves,
They'll tickle your nose and cause you to sneeze!
In this fruity realm where giggles bloom,
Nature's laughter fills every room.

Nectar Dripping from Elation

In the garden, joy does drip,
From blossoms taking a laughter sip.
Nectar flows like a silly stream,
Pouring giggles in a sunlit dream.

Bees in bowties zoom around,
With tiny trumpets, they share their sound.
The flowers chuckle, waving their dyes,
As butterflies perform their playful highs.

Tulips with socks and daffodils in hats,
Join in dances with the giddy cats.
Each drop of nectar a sweet, funny joke,
While frogs croak along, making folks poke.

A party blooms in each sunny ray,
Cheering up clouds that drift and play.
With nectar's sweetness, hearts all lift,
In the garden of joy, life's the best gift.

A Symphony of Melodic Hues

A rainbow spreads its arms quite wide,
As fruits and flowers jolly abide.
The colors laugh, a playful scene,
In this symphony, cheerful and keen.

Frilly oranges hum a tune,
While purple grapes sway under the moon.
Every shade joins in the fun,
As their vibrant coats shine like the sun.

The cherries quack like silly ducks,
While the peas joke about veggie trucks.
Fruits form bands with plucky zest,
Creating melodies that simply jest.

In this concert of joy, no notes are missed,
Each giggle and chuckle by the fruits kissed.
Together they burst with colorful glee,
A harmonious romp of nature's spree.

Swaying Dreams in the Gentle Breeze

In the gentle sway, dreams take flight,
With every rustle, laughter ignites.
The leaves giggle in a playful dance,
While the wind whispers secrets, giving a glance.

The fruit hang low, just waiting to tease,
With puns wrapped up in soft summer breeze.
Plums roll their eyes, having their fun,
While chatter erupts in the warm golden sun.

Coconuts play hide and seek with the sky,
As blushing peaches say a sweet goodbye.
Banquets of nectar tease buzzing bees,
Nature's fiesta amidst the trees.

Underneath the sky so vast and true,
The orchard revels in a silly view.
With every sway, laughter spreads wide,
In the breezy haven, pure joy does abide.

The Chronicles of Sweetness

In the jungle, a fruit did dance,
A yellow delight, in a leafy prance.
With a laugh so bright, it swung with glee,
Chasing the shadows, wild and free.

The monkeys join in a funny cheer,
While squirrels giggle, oh dear, oh dear!
A slip, a slide, and they all fall down,
Rolling in joy, a colorful crown.

Everyone loves this cheerful treat,
Dressed in pajamas, oh what a feat!
In the sun they squawk and grin,
For this ripe laughter is the sweetest win.

So let's toast the night with fruity song,
A tale of joy, where all belong.
In a world where flavors burst and bloom,
Laughter and sweetness chase away gloom.

Serenade of Spheres

A jolly fruit with a loud parade,
On a sunny day, they laugh and played.
With polka dots and hats on their heads,
These playful spheres tumble from their beds.

They roll and bounce in a merry chase,
Wobbling round with a cheerful grace.
A monkey tries to catch the fun,
But slips and lands with a thud, then runs.

The brassy birds chirp in delight,
As the sunshine twinkles, oh so bright.
A fruity serenade fills the air,
As giggles stir, with a flair to spare.

So let's dance under the leafy shade,
With joyous fruit, never to fade.
Each giggle shared is a vibrant tune,
In this silly world of joy, we swoon.

Journey Through the Canopy

High above where the breezes sing,
A twisty road for a fruity fling.
With slippery paths, they take a ride,
Hiding from shadows, full of pride.

A squirrel squeaks at a juicy sight,
With silly moves, they dance in flight.
Branches crackle under their glee,
As they tumble down, oh woe is me!

Each swing buzzes with a joyful cheer,
As laughter echoes from ear to ear.
The jungle's rhythm sets the pace,
For every twist in this fruity race.

The sun peeks through the leafy trails,
As nature spins its funny tales.
And in this canopy of delight,
The journey keeps us laughing bright.

Colorful Delights

In a patch of sunshine, colors collide,
A medley of giggles, a joyful ride.
With speckled spots and a shiny smile,
These fruity wonders dance in style.

A banana parade with dazzling flair,
Tickling the toes of those who dare.
From oranges, lemons join in the fun,
Messy and playful, they're never done.

"Wobble with me," calls a bright pink pear,
"Jiggle and giggle without a care!"
With each bounce, the colors fade,
As laughter ignites a joyous cascade.

So let your heart feel the fruity beat,
In this vibrant world, oh what a treat!
With every giggle, our spirits delight,
In a banquet of fun, from day to night.

Colorful Horizons

In the garden, bright and bold,
The fruits wear hats of green and gold.
They dance and sway in sunlit cheer,
With giggles echoing far and near.

Beneath the leaves, a monkey swings,
Wearing laughter, oh, the joy it brings!
With silly faces, they take their stance,
In this fruity, jovial romance.

The breeze whispers secrets, sweet and light,
As colors swirl in a playful flight.
Jokes are tossed like seeds on ground,
In this land where silliness is found.

A parade of flavors come to play,
In a funny, fruity cabaret.
Each smile ripens, ripe for the show,
In the sunny fields where giggles grow.

A Tapestry of Flavor

A yellow cap on a jester's head,
Sways with rhythm, it's fun instead.
With each twist, the laughter bursts,
Creating joy, oh, how it thirsts!

A fruit walks by in a funky dance,
With every wobble, it takes a chance.
Splashes of color in every shade,
In a merry fruit parade displayed.

Tickled pink is the fuzzy peach,
Telling stories that tickle and teach.
As the pineapple spins in delight,
Fruity fables bloom in the light.

This tapestry woven with zest and glee,
Is a fruity festival for all to see.
With giggles aplenty and joy galore,
It's a canvas of flavors, forever to explore.

Radiance Underfoot

The ground is ripe with funny sights,
As nature slips in joyful bites.
A playful crowd of colors wake,
With every step, a giggle to make.

The little fruit with a silly grin,
Shimmies and shakes, a joyous spin.
With shoes made of zest, they prance about,
In this world, you cannot pout!

Beneath the leaves, the laughter grows,
In the patch, where silliness flows.
Giggling roots tickle the ground,
With each chuckle, new joy is found.

So take a stroll where flavors meet,
And let the fruity fun be sweet.
In every corner, a joke to catch,
A bright, funny world, in nature's patch.

Fruity Fables

Once upon a vine so sweet,
The fruits conspired to dance and greet.
In a realm where the colors glow,
Laughter ripens, just so you know.

A cheeky lemon cracks a joke,
While berries giggle with each poke.
In the orchard, stories unfold,
Of silly twists and tastes untold.

The kiwi wears a silly hat,
While the cherry rolls, oh, just like that!
In a frolic, the fruits unite,
Creating tales that feel just right.

With every nibble, joy invades,
As fruity fables make their raids.
In this land of humor and zest,
Nature's laughter truly is the best.

Joyful Abundance Unfold

In a jungle of laughter, they peek,
Green crescents giggle, so unique.
They wear coats of sunshine, quite bold,
Whispers of sweetness, stories untold.

Ticklish branches sway with delight,
Fruits making faces, what a sight!
Giddy friends frolic in the sun,
Nature's jesters, a fruit-filled fun.

Giant leaves dance, a silly parade,
Each step a wiggle, no plans made.
From puddles of pollen, they spring,
Silly antics of the ripening ring.

With giggles echoing through the trees,
Who knew ripe joy could be so breezy?
Duck and dodge as the harvest rolls,
Jovial treasures, a feast for souls.

Swaying in the Breeze

Bouncing bobbles hang in a row,
Swinging to tunes only they know.
Cousins of chaos, swirling around,
What kind of mischief will they compound?

Sunshine tickles, with a playful nudge,
Leaves rustle laughter, can't help but judge!
Popping out giggles under the blue,
Silly surprises that's all they do.

Floating whispers, a fruity ballet,
As shadows shimmy through the sunny ray.
Round and round, the frolic begins,
With each gentle sway, mischief spins.

Chasing the breeze, what a ride!
These goofy hangers swing, wide-eyed.
Nature's clowns in their leaf-clad glee,
With every twist, they laugh with glee.

Untamed by the Seasons

In wild wonder, they hop and hop,
Giggling in spring when the rain won't stop.
Summer spins laughter, with cheeks aglow,
Autumn's confetti, a colorful show.

Frosty mornings give no warning,
Yet still they grin at the early dawning.
Festive frolic, a year-round tease,
Flavorful fun in the softest breeze.

Beneath the branches, the parties bloom,
Teasing the sky with their fruity plume.
Rolling along with the playful air,
Tickled with joy, free from despair.

Winter may come, but their spirits soar,
Jolly and bright, who could ask for more?
Each season's a painter with fruity strokes,
Clicking their heels, the sun always pokes!

Lush Landscapes Unfurling

In a canvas of green, laughter takes flight,
Colors collide in the warm daylight.
Sassy shapes tumble, giggles ensue,
Nature's own jesters, dancing anew.

Around twinkling trees, the joy takes form,
As critters collect in a giggliest swarm.
Whirling whispers, smoothie of cheer,
A party of flavors, oh how they steer!

Bouncing like balls on a joyful spree,
Fruitful delights hanging carefree.
Rain sings a melody, sweet and light,
While shadows shimmy, oh what a sight!

Sprightly scenes with a fruity twist,
Adventure beckons, can't be missed.
The fill of the air with a playful rhyme,
Full of life, oh what a sublime!

Sunshine's Golden Kiss

In a garden full of glee,
Yellow hats sway like sea.
Bunches chuckle, oh what fun,
Joking with the honest sun.

Skins so bright, like silly pears,
Swinging low without a care.
Laughter ripples through the trees,
Dancing leaves in gentle breeze.

Fruity giggles, oh so sweet,
Tickled toes and happy feet.
Welcome warmth, the sunshine's hug,
Silly fruits, they do a tug.

With each ray, a wink is cast,
Fruity moods will ever last.
So we grin, stand tall and proud,
Nature's jesters call out loud.

Tropical Symphonies

In a land of zesty cheer,
Treetops play a tune so dear.
Boys in yellow do a dance,
With sunshine, they take a chance.

Each bright fruit sings a note,
Hanging high, like a funny boat.
A symphony of laughter rings,
Joyful whispers on the wings.

Green leaves sway to every beat,
Tropical fun can't be beat.
As the breeze plays waves of sound,
Lying under joyfully found.

With each strum, the sun beams wide,
Nature's jesters slip and slide.
Come join in, the tune's alive,
Where giggles and green dreams thrive.

Nature's Gilded Tapestry

In the garden, laughter spools,
Bright fibers twist like playful fools.
Woven tales of yellow cheer,
Nature's scarf wrapped round the year.

Hanging bright, like jokes unspun,
Kites of color chase the sun.
Each twist and turn in the air,
Makes us giggle in the fair.

Fruit of laughter, serenades,
Gilded gowns in evening shades.
Swaying whimsies, soft and light,
Chasing shadows into night.

In this weave of giggly glee,
Nature's story sings with thee.
Tapestries of joy are found,
Playful whispers all around.

Ripening in Harmony

In the orchard, laughter swells,
Fruits in chorus, funny bells.
Hanging low with playful swing,
Their sweet secrets make us sing.

As they ripen, jokes unfold,
Colors bright, a sight to behold.
Silly smiles from branch to ground,
Joyful whispers all around.

Nature's giggle, warm and bright,
Beneath the watchful sun's delight.
With every peel, a laugh erupts,
Life's humor gently interrupts.

Ripening slowly, humor's grace,
Fruity puns in every place.
Join the dance, let's all partake,
In this laughter, we shall wake.

Sun-Kissed Fruit and Verdant Dreams

In the garden's sunny delight,
Yellow hats in full flight.
Swinging softly in the breeze,
They giggle, flutter, and tease.

Round and merry, they're a sight,
Dancing in the warm sunlight.
A monkey's laugh, a joyful sound,
In this fruity playground found.

Peeling layers, oh so sly,
Chasing shadows in the sky.
They bounce along with playful glee,
Nature's jesters, wild and free.

In a smoothie, they might hide,
With cream and fun, full of pride.
A splash of joy, a zing so bright,
They're the stars of every bite.

Laughing Leaves and Spiky Colors

Leaves are gossiping away,
Underneath the sunny sway.
Blades of green with cheeky grins,
Tickling each other as the fun begins.

Spiky friends in sunny coats,
Wearing laughter like bright notes.
Funky hats and wild surprise,
Blooming joy beneath the skies.

With the breeze, they spin and sway,
Dramatic moves, a leafy ballet.
Colors shouting, shades so bold,
Stories in the garden told.

Nature's jesters, wild and loud,
Join the sun, they dance so proud.
With every rustle, cheer they send,
For every bud, a leafy friend.

Harvest of the Sun's Embrace

Golden treasures hang about,
In the sun, they twist and shout.
Crowned in laughter, round and bright,
They glow with joy, oh what a sight!

Tickled pink in morning's rays,
Waving hands in funny ways.
A chorus sung by nature's choir,
Creating cheer, a playful fire.

In the basket, dreams arise,
Sweet delights, a grand surprise.
Bouncing, rolling in a race,
Every globe a smiling face.

With a crunch, the joy explodes,
In sweet bites, the laughter loads.
Harvest time, a happy spree,
Nature's treats, for you and me!

Whispers of the Tropics

Whispers float on balmy air,
Tropical tales of laughter and flair.
Fruits that giggle on the vine,
Swaying tales in sunshine's shine.

A sunny party, wild and grand,
Jumpy plants in a gleeful band.
With each rustle, secrets spread,
Of wiggles, wiggles in their bed.

Bunches swing with comic ties,
In the breeze, their humor flies.
Juba jubilee in green parade,
The chortling leaves, a happy charade.

In the tropics, laughter rings,
Dappled light where the sunshine sings.
Join the dance, let's be a part,
Of nature's festival, a joyful heart!

Peel Back the Layers

Beneath the yellow skin we find,
A treasure hidden, a sweet kind.
Slip on the peel, what a surprise!
Life's a comedy in disguise!

Twist and turn, the fruit's awake,
Find the sweetness, for heaven's sake!
Fascination with every bite,
A giggle in the morning light!

Chasing monkeys, we take flight,
Swinging high, oh, what a sight!
Nature's joke, ripe laughs abound,
In this tropical playground!

So peel away, unleash the cheer,
A funny fruit that brings good cheer.
Come one, come all, have a bite,
Let's dance and laugh into the night!

Bounty of the Tropics

Upon the vine, a circus grows,
In shades of yellow, a fun show!
Pineapples strut, coconuts sway,
As laughter frolics in the sun's ray.

A feast awaits beneath the trees,
Swinging low with the gentle breeze.
Kooky fruit, oh to indulge,
Bring out the fork, let's not bulge!

Monkey business, what a sight,
Climbing high, they're full of bite!
With hats of leaves and shoes of vine,
They giggle and dance, quite divine!

Join the party, what a thrill,
Bring your snacks and bring your will.
In this land of endless cheer,
The bounty's ripe, the laughter near!

Mesmerizing Yellow

A golden hue that catches eyes,
With every curve, it's a surprise.
Peel it back, take a taste,
In this joy, there's no haste!

Chattering critters come to feast,
In tropic sun, they munch the least.
Dancing shadows on the ground,
In this delight, pure joy is found.

Silly faces in the sun,
Chasing fruit is all in fun!
Fruitful laughter fills the air,
Worries vanish, without a care.

All around, the giggles flow,
Wrap your heart in this yellow glow.
It's a world where smiles bloom,
Let's celebrate, dispel the gloom!

The Dance of Fruition

In tropical climes, where laughter roams,
Fruits gather, building their homes.
Yellow hats on leafy heads,
Swaying gently, where joy spreads.

Jumpy critters join the show,
In a quickstep, to and fro.
Ripened treasures, quirky delights,
Sparkling joy on sunny nights.

The wacky fruit finds its groove,
In the rhythm, they all move.
Twirling, jumping, what a spree,
This joyful dance, so wild and free!

Come one, come all, take a chance,
In the rhythm of nature's dance.
Let's celebrate every bite,
In this fun-filled fruity night!

www.ingramcontent.com/pod-product-compliance
Lightning Source LLC
Chambersburg PA
CBHW071126130526
44590CB00056B/2544